SELLING BEYOND LIMITS:

BREAKTHROUGH STRATEGIES FOR SALES TRIUMPH

Table Of Contents

INTRODUCTION

Welcome to a transformative journey that transcends the conventional boundaries of sales literature. "Selling Beyond Limits: Breakthrough Strategies for Sales Triumph" isn't just an eBook; it's an indispensable guide that unlocks the secrets to mastering the art and science of sales. As you stand at the threshold of this immersive experience, let's explore the profound importance of not just buying but delving into the pages of this eBook.

Beyond the Ordinary: A Guided Expedition into Sales Mastery

Elevating Your Sales Game

In a world saturated with generic sales advice, "Selling Beyond Limits" stands as a beacon of authenticity. It is not merely a compilation of well-worn tactics; it's a guided expedition into the heart of sales mastery. Whether you're a seasoned professional seeking to elevate your sales game or a newcomer eager to grasp the fundamentals, this eBook offers a fresh perspective that transcends the ordinary.

A Symphony of Expertise

Crafted by seasoned professionals and industry experts, each chapter resonates with a symphony of expertise. The blend of theoretical knowledge and practical wisdom creates a harmonious narrative that isn't just informative but deeply insightful. This isn't just a how-to guide; it's a journey into the nuanced dynamics of sales, where every page offers a gem of wisdom to enrich your approach.

Unraveling the Layers: Why It Matters

A Comprehensive Toolkit for Success

"Selling Beyond Limits" is not a one-size-fits-all solution. It's a comprehensive toolkit that caters to the diverse needs of sales professionals across the spectrum. Each chapter unfolds like a layer of insight, equipping you with strategies tailored for various situations. It's not just about closing deals; it's about crafting enduring relationships, navigating the digital landscape, and mastering the art of negotiation – a holistic approach to sales success.

Navigating the Contemporary Sales Landscape

The dynamics of sales are ever-evolving, shaped by technological advancements, changing consumer behaviors, and global market shifts. This eBook serves as your compass in navigating this intricate landscape. It's a guide that doesn't just echo traditional wisdom but adapts it to the demands of the digital era. As the sales landscape transforms, "Selling Beyond Limits" keeps you ahead of the curve.

Your Personalized Sales Mentor

Beyond Generic Advice

Unlike generic advice that leaves you searching for practical applications, "Selling Beyond Limits" is your personalized mentor. It doesn't just tell you what to do; it shows you how to do it. Each chapter is a mentorship session, offering actionable insights and real-world strategies that you can implement immediately. It's a companion that understands the intricacies of your journey and provides tailored guidance.

Building a Foundation for Lifelong Success

The importance of this eBook extends beyond immediate gains. It lays the foundation for lifelong success in the field of sales. From understanding the psychology of buyers to mastering the art of negotiation and embracing continuous learning, the lessons imparted here are not just for today's transactions but for building a resilient and enduring career.

Investing in Your Professional Growth

Beyond a Transaction: An Investment in Yourself

When you invest in "Selling Beyond Limits," you're not just making a transaction; you're investing in yourself. The insights contained within these pages are catalysts for personal and professional growth. They empower you to transcend limitations, break through barriers, and redefine what's possible in your sales career. It's an investment that yields returns far beyond the cost of the eBook.

A Transformative Experience

Consider this eBook not just as a read but as a transformative experience. It's a journey that challenges, inspires, and equips you to rise above the ordinary. As you immerse yourself in the pages of "Selling Beyond Limits," anticipate a shift in mindset, a refinement of skills, and a renewed enthusiasm for the art of selling.

The Journey Awaits

In conclusion, the importance of buying and reading "Selling Beyond Limits: Breakthrough Strategies for Sales Triumph" extends beyond acquiring knowledge; it's about embarking on a journey of self-discovery and professional mastery. The keys to sales success are within reach, and this eBook is your guide to unlocking them. The journey awaits – turn the page and step into a world where your sales potential knows no limits.

THE FOUNDATION OF SALES MASTERY

In the intricate dance of sales, success is not merely a transaction; it's an art form, a science, and a deeply nuanced understanding of the human psyche. To embark on the journey of sales mastery, we must first delve into the intricate tapestry of the psychology that governs both buyers and sellers. As we unravel the threads of cognition, emotion, and decision-making, a profound comprehension emerges, laying the groundwork for unparalleled sales triumph.

Understanding the Psychology of Buyers and Sellers

The Dance of Decision-Making

Picture this: a potential buyer perusing your product or service. What influences their decision to make a purchase? The answer lies in the intricate workings of their psyche. This section explores the psychological triggers that initiate and guide the decision-making process. From the initial spark of interest to the final commitment, we dissect the factors that sway the buyer's mind, offering keen insights for a strategic approach.

Understanding Emotional Triggers: Unravel the emotional landscape that drives decision-making. Explore how joy, fear, desire, and urgency can be harnessed to create compelling narratives that resonate with your audience.

The Role of Cognitive Biases: Dive into the world of cognitive biases that shape perceptions and choices. Learn how to navigate biases such as anchoring, confirmation bias, and loss aversion to your advantage in the sales arena.

Building Trust through Psychology: Trust is the currency of successful sales. Explore techniques to establish trust through understanding the psychological elements that contribute to a buyer's sense of security and confidence.

Crafting Persuasive Narratives

In the realm of sales, stories are more than anecdotes—they are powerful tools that resonate with the human experience. This section focuses on the art of storytelling as a means to captivate and persuade your audience.

The Hero's Journey in Sales: Explore the hero's journey framework and how it can be applied to the sales narrative. Position your product or service as the guide that helps customers overcome challenges and achieve their goals.

Storytelling Techniques for Emotional Connection: Delve into storytelling techniques that evoke emotion and foster a deep connection between your brand and the buyer. Learn how to craft narratives that leave a lasting impression.

Building a Resilient Mindset for Sales Success

The Power of Positivity

In the often turbulent waters of sales, a resilient mindset is the anchor that keeps professionals steady. This section explores the psychology of resilience and positivity, providing tools to navigate challenges and setbacks with grace.

Embracing a Growth Mindset: Learn how a growth mindset can transform challenges into opportunities for learning and development. Understand the difference between a fixed and growth mindset and how it shapes success in sales.

Overcoming Rejection and Adversity: Rejection is an inherent part of sales. Discover strategies to bounce back from rejection, turning it into a catalyst for improvement and future success.

The Psychology of Confidence: Confidence is magnetic. Explore techniques to cultivate and exude confidence in your sales interactions. Understand the delicate balance between humility and self-assuredness.

Mindfulness in Sales

In the fast-paced world of sales, mindfulness is a superpower. This section explores the intersection of mindfulness and sales success, offering practical techniques to stay present, focused, and effective.

The Art of Active Listening: Master the skill of active listening to truly understand your customers' needs and concerns. Learn how being fully present in the moment enhances your ability to connect with clients.

Mindfulness Techniques for Stress Reduction: Explore mindfulness practices that alleviate stress and promote mental clarity. Understand how a centered and composed mindset contributes to effective decision-making.

UNLEASHING YOUR UNIQUE SELLING PROPOSITION (USP)

In the vast landscape of commerce, where countless products and services vie for attention, the discerning sales professional must wield a powerful weapon—the Unique Selling Proposition (USP). This chapter delves into the strategic art of crafting a compelling value proposition and uncovering the distinctive advantages that set your offering apart in the competitive arena.

Crafting a Compelling Value Proposition

The Essence of Value

At the heart of every successful sale lies a value proposition that speaks directly to the needs and desires of the customer. This section navigates the nuances of crafting a value proposition that resonates, exploring the art of articulating what makes your product or service indispensable.

Customer-Centric Value Creation: Dive into the minds of your customers to understand their pain points, desires, and aspirations. Learn how to align your value proposition with the specific needs of your target audience.

Clarity and Conciseness: Hone the art of communicating your value proposition with clarity and conciseness. Explore techniques to distill complex offerings into clear and compelling messages that capture attention.

Quantifiable Value Metrics: Develop metrics to quantify the value your product or service delivers. Showcase tangible benefits, whether they be cost savings, time efficiency, or unique features that differentiate your offering.

Emotional Resonance in Value Propositions

Beyond the rational, successful value propositions tap into the emotional realm. This section explores the power of emotional resonance, uncovering how to forge connections that go beyond features and benefits.

Evoking Emotion Through Storytelling: Integrate storytelling into your value proposition to create an emotional connection with your audience. Explore case studies and narratives that showcase the positive impact of your offering on customers.

Appealing to Aspirations: Understand the aspirations and dreams of your target audience. Learn how to position your product or service as a vehicle for customers to achieve their goals and aspirations.

Identifying and Leveraging Your Competitive Advantages

The Competitive Landscape

To stand out, one must first understand the competitive terrain. This section guides you through the process of conducting a comprehensive analysis of your competitors, allowing you to identify and leverage your unique strengths.

SWOT Analysis for Strategic Insight: Conduct a thorough SWOT (Strengths, Weaknesses, Opportunities, Threats) analysis to gain strategic insights into your business. Identify areas where you excel and uncover opportunities for differentiation.

Differentiation Strategies: Explore various strategies for differentiation, from product innovation to service excellence. Understand how to position your offering in a way that not only sets it apart but also creates a sustainable competitive advantage.

Building on Core Competencies: Identify and leverage your organization's core competencies. Learn how to align these strengths with the needs of your target market to create a formidable competitive edge.

Communicating Competitive Advantages Effectively

Possessing a competitive advantage is one thing; effectively communicating it is another. This section equips you with the skills to convey your unique strengths persuasively.

Crafting a Unique Value Proposition Statement: Develop a concise and impactful value proposition statement that encapsulates your competitive advantages. Learn how to articulate it consistently across various communication channels.

Visual and Verbal Branding: Explore the role of visual and verbal branding in reinforcing your unique selling proposition. Understand how design elements, messaging, and branding materials contribute to a cohesive and compelling brand image.

THE ART OF EFFECTIVE COMMUNICATION IN SALES

In the domain of deals, where each cooperation is a fragile dance among influence and association, becoming the best at compelling correspondence is principal. This section leaves on an excursion through the complexities of enticing correspondence, revealing the methods that change an attempt to seal the deal into a convincing story. Besides, we dive into the frequently misjudged expertise of undivided attention — a central component for building more grounded, more significant associations with clients.

Dominating the Force of Convincing Correspondence

The Underpinnings of Influence

To convince is to guide, impact, and move activity. In this part, we investigate the mental groundworks of influence, analyzing the components that make correspondence effective as well as overwhelming.

The Influence Standards: Reveal the rules that underlie influential correspondence, from Robert

Cialdini's standards of impact to Aristotle's ethos, tenderness, and logos. Figure out how to apply these standards morally to upgrade the influence of your messages.

Making Convincing Messages: Plunge into the specialty of creating messages that reverberate with your crowd. Figure out the significance of lucidity, effortlessness, and close to home reverberation in making messages that have an enduring effect.

Adjusting to Various Correspondence Styles: Investigate assorted correspondence styles and how they reverberate with various character types. Foster the capacity to adjust your correspondence way to deal with interface all the more really with different clients.

The Job of Non-Verbal Correspondence
Correspondence stretches out indeed. This segment digs into the nuanced universe of non-verbal signs, investigating how non-verbal communication, looks, and motions add to the general effect of your message.

Non-verbal communication Dominance: Figure out the meaning of non-verbal communication in correspondence. Figure out how to convey certainty, receptiveness, and earnestness through essential non-verbal communication, improving your generally powerful presence.

Visual and Vocal Components: Investigate the visual and vocal parts of correspondence, from your manner of speaking to the utilization of visual guides. Find how these components add to the general influence of your correspondence.

Making a Predictable Brand Picture: Adjust your correspondence style with your image picture. Figure out how consistency in correspondence supports your image personality, building trust and acknowledgment with your crowd.

Undivided attention Methods for Building More grounded Associations

The Specialty of Presence
While influence is a craftsmanship, undivided attention is the foundation of significant associations. This segment investigates the groundbreaking force of really tuning in — drawing in with your clients in a way that goes beyond anything describable.

Groundworks of Undivided attention: Handle the essential standards of undivided attention. Grasp the significance of concentration, receptiveness, and compassion in establishing a climate helpful for significant correspondence.

Intelligent Listening Procedures: Become the best at intelligent tuning in, a procedure that includes rewording and summing up to exhibit understanding. Investigate how this strategy encourages further associations and explains correspondence.

Addressing Methodologies for Keen Discussions: Figure out how to ask strong, genuine inquiries that urge clients to share their contemplations, needs, and concerns. Comprehend how insightful addressing adds to a more significant comprehension of your clients.

Exploring Difficulties in Correspondence
Correspondence isn't without its difficulties. This part tends to normal snags in the deals correspondence process and gives procedures to beating them.

Taking care of Protests with Compassion: Investigate procedures for tending to protests with sympathy and understanding. Figure out how to transform protests into potential open doors for explanation and influence.

Overseeing Errors and Miscommunications: Dive into procedures for forestalling and settling mistaken assumptions. Grasp the job of clearness, affirmation, and criticism in alleviating potential correspondence traps.

Incorporating Convincing Correspondence and Undivided attention
In the last section of this part, we unite the specialty of powerful correspondence and the ability of undivided attention. Find how these two components synergize to make a dynamic and effective deals correspondence system.

Making a Convincing Story: Investigate how undivided attention illuminates and upgrades your capacity to make an influential story. Comprehend how experiences acquired through mindful listening can be woven into your directives for more noteworthy effect.

Constructing Long haul Connections through Correspondence: Perceive the job of compelling correspondence in encouraging long haul associations with clients. Figure out how steady, open, and compassionate correspondence adds to client steadfastness and fulfillment.

NAVIGATING THE SALES FUNNEL WITH PRECISION

In the dynamic landscape of sales, where prospects transition through distinct stages, mastering the navigation of the sales funnel is essential for success. This chapter is dedicated to unveiling strategies that elevate your approach to prospecting and lead generation, ensuring a seamless transition from initial interest to cultivating loyal, long-term customers.

Strategies for Prospecting and Lead Generation

Understanding the Dynamics of Prospecting

Prospecting is the gateway to the sales journey, where potential opportunities are identified and nurtured. This section explores strategic approaches to prospecting that go beyond the surface, uncovering opportunities that align with your offerings.

Targeted Prospecting Techniques: Delve into targeted prospecting strategies that focus on identifying prospects who align with your ideal customer profile. Learn how to leverage data, market research, and customer personas to refine your prospecting efforts.

Multi-Channel Prospecting: Explore the advantages of a multi-channel prospecting approach. Understand how combining various channels such as social media, email, and networking events can amplify your reach and engagement with potential leads.

Building Strategic Alliances for Referrals: Investigate the power of strategic alliances and partnerships in prospecting. Learn how to build relationships that result in valuable referrals, expanding your network and prospect pool.

Crafting Compelling Lead Magnets

Once prospects are identified, the next step is to capture their attention with compelling lead magnets. This section delves into the art of creating irresistible incentives that encourage potential customers to take the next step in the sales journey.

Creating High-Value Content Offers: Explore the creation of content offers that provide genuine value to your prospects. Learn how to align content with their needs, addressing pain points and offering solutions that position your brand as an authority.

Interactive Lead Magnets and Quizzes: Embrace interactive lead magnets and quizzes as engaging tools for lead generation. Understand how these dynamic elements not only capture attention but also provide valuable insights into prospect preferences and needs.

Converting Leads into Loyal Customers

Nurturing Leads with Strategic Engagement

Successfully navigating the sales funnel requires a nuanced approach to lead nurturing. This section delves into the importance of strategic engagement to guide leads through the journey from interest to commitment.

Automated Lead Nurturing Campaigns: Explore the benefits of automated lead nurturing campaigns. Understand how automated workflows can deliver timely and relevant content to leads, fostering engagement and maintaining top-of-mind awareness.

Personalized Communication Strategies: Implement personalized communication strategies that resonate with individual leads. Learn how to leverage data and insights to tailor your messages, creating a more meaningful connection with prospects.

Strategies for Overcoming Objections: Address common objections and concerns during the lead nurturing process. Equip yourself with strategies to build trust and provide information that addresses potential barriers to conversion.

Closing the Deal: Effective Sales Strategies

The culmination of effective lead generation is the conversion of prospects into customers. This section explores strategies for closing deals with finesse and ensuring a smooth transition from interest to commitment.

Strategic Follow-Up Techniques: Develop strategic follow-up techniques to maintain momentum and guide prospects toward the decision-making stage. Understand the balance between persistence and patience in follow-up communications.

Closing Techniques for Various Scenarios: Explore a repertoire of closing techniques tailored to different scenarios. From consultative selling to assumptive closing, adapt your approach based on the unique needs and preferences of your prospects.

Integrating Prospecting and Conversion Strategies

In the final segment of this chapter, we bring together the strategies for prospecting and converting leads into a cohesive and dynamic sales funnel. Discover how a well-orchestrated approach enhances the overall effectiveness of your sales process.

Measuring and Analyzing Funnel Performance: Implement metrics and analytics to measure the performance of your sales funnel. Learn how to identify strengths and weaknesses in your process, enabling continuous improvement and optimization.

Creating a Seamless Customer Journey: Understand the importance of creating a seamless and enjoyable customer journey. From the first touchpoint to the final conversion, ensure that each step contributes to a positive and memorable experience for your customers.

ADVANCED TECHNIQUES IN RELATIONSHIP BUILDING

In the dynamic world of sales, relationships are the cornerstone of long-term success. This chapter delves into advanced techniques for relationship building, focusing on the critical aspects of establishing trust and credibility while nurturing enduring connections that transcend individual transactions.

Establishing Trust and Credibility

The Foundation of Successful Relationships

Trust and credibility are the bedrock upon which enduring relationships are built. In this section, we explore the intricate dynamics of trust-building and how establishing credibility lays the groundwork for meaningful connections.

Authenticity as a Trust Accelerator: Uncover the power of authenticity in building trust. Explore how being genuine, transparent, and true to your values creates a foundation for trust that resonates with clients.

Consistency and Reliability: Delve into the role of consistency and reliability in establishing trust. Learn how delivering on promises, meeting deadlines, and maintaining a reliable presence contribute to building trust over time.

Transparency in Communication: Explore the art of transparent communication. Understand how open and honest communication, even in challenging situations, fosters trust and strengthens the foundation of your client relationships.

Building Credibility Through Expertise

Credibility is earned through expertise and a deep understanding of your field. This section delves into strategies for showcasing your knowledge and positioning yourself as a trusted authority.

Thought Leadership Strategies: Embrace thought leadership as a strategy for building credibility. Learn how to share insights, industry trends, and innovative ideas through various channels to establish yourself as a go-to expert.

Continuous Learning and Skill Development: Stay ahead in your field by prioritizing continuous learning and skill development. Explore how expanding your expertise not only enhances your credibility but also positions you as an invaluable resource for clients.

Creating Long-Term Client Relationships

Beyond Transactions: The Client-Centric Approach

Long-term relationships extend beyond individual transactions. This section explores the shift toward a client-centric approach that focuses on understanding and meeting the evolving needs of your clients.

Understanding Client Needs and Goals: Dive into strategies for understanding the unique needs and goals of your clients. Learn how active listening, client surveys, and regular check-ins contribute to a deeper understanding of their evolving priorities.

Tailoring Solutions to Individual Clients: Explore the art of tailoring your solutions to the specific needs of individual clients. Understand how customization and personalization enhance the value you provide, fostering a sense of partnership.

Effective Communication in Relationship Building

Communication is the lifeblood of any relationship. This section delves into advanced communication techniques that go beyond the basics, fostering stronger connections with clients.

Strategic Client Communication Plans: Develop strategic communication plans for each client. Explore the importance of regular touchpoints, status updates, and proactive communication in building a robust and communicative relationship.

Handling Feedback and Resolving Issues: Learn how to handle feedback, both positive and constructive, in a way that strengthens your relationship. Explore strategies for resolving issues promptly and maintaining a positive rapport.

Nurturing Relationships Through Value-Added Services

To solidify long-term relationships, providing value beyond the core offering is paramount. This section explores strategies for offering value-added services that enhance the client experience.

Surprise and Delight Strategies: Delve into surprise and delight strategies that exceed client expectations. Explore how unexpected gestures, exclusive offers, and personalized experiences contribute to a positive and memorable client journey.

Anticipating Client Needs: Develop the ability to anticipate and address client needs before they arise. Understand the role of proactive problem-solving and foresight in creating a seamless and satisfying client experience.

Integrating Trust-Building and Relationship Nurturing

In the final segment of this chapter, we bring together the advanced techniques in trust-building and relationship nurturing into a cohesive strategy. Discover how combining these elements elevates your approach to relationship building and contributes to sustained success.

Creating a Relationship Roadmap: Develop a roadmap for each client relationship, outlining key touchpoints, goals, and strategies for trust-building and value delivery. Understand how a structured approach contributes to the long-term success of your client relationships.

Measuring Relationship Health: Implement metrics to measure the health of your client relationships. Explore indicators of trust, satisfaction, and loyalty, enabling you to proactively address any potential challenges and capitalize on opportunities for growth.

CLOSING STRATEGIES FOR EVERY SITUATION

In the intricate dance of sales, the art of closing deals is the grand finale—a culmination of strategic maneuvers, persuasive finesse, and a deep understanding of your client's needs. This chapter is dedicated to exploring a repertoire of closing strategies for every situation, equipping you with the skills to overcome common objections and employ trial closes that lead to the successful finalization of deals.

Overcoming Common Objections

Understanding the Psychology of Objections

Objections are a natural part of the sales process, often signaling potential areas of concern for the client. This section delves into the psychology of objections, exploring why they arise and how to navigate them effectively.

Turning Objections into Opportunities: Develop a mindset that views objections as opportunities for clarification and understanding. Learn how to approach objections with curiosity and empathy, turning potential roadblocks into stepping stones towards closing the deal.

Common Types of Objections and Their Solutions: Explore common objections in sales scenarios and effective strategies for addressing each type. From pricing concerns to product specifications, equip yourself with tailored responses that instill confidence in your clients.

Building Trust During Objection Handling

The way objections are handled can either strengthen or weaken the client's trust. This section explores techniques for maintaining trust and credibility even in the face of objections.

Active Listening in Objection Handling: Elevate your objection-handling skills through active listening. Understand how attentive listening not only allows you to fully comprehend objections but also demonstrates your commitment to understanding and addressing client concerns.

Empathetic Responses to Objections: Cultivate empathy in your responses to objections. Learn how to acknowledge and validate client concerns, fostering a sense of understanding and partnership in the resolution process.

Trial Closes and Techniques for Finalizing Deals

The Art of the Trial Close

Trial closes are strategic checkpoints in the sales process that gauge the client's readiness to move forward. This section explores the art of trial closes and how they can be seamlessly integrated into your interactions.

Types of Trial Closes: Explore various trial close techniques, from assumptive trial closes to alternative choice closes. Understand how each type serves as a valuable indicator of the client's level of commitment and readiness to proceed.

Reading Buying Signals: Hone your ability to read subtle buying signals during trial closes. Learn to interpret verbal and non-verbal cues that indicate the client's receptiveness to the proposed solution, allowing you to tailor your approach accordingly.

Finalizing Deals with Confidence

Closing the deal is the culmination of a well-executed sales process. This section delves into strategies for finalizing deals with confidence, ensuring a smooth transition from discussions to agreements.

Creating a Sense of Urgency: Explore the psychology of urgency and how it can be strategically employed to encourage timely decision-making. Learn how to communicate deadlines and incentives that motivate clients to move forward.

Addressing Final Questions and Concerns: Navigate the final stages of deal finalization by addressing any remaining questions or concerns. Develop a comprehensive approach to ensure that clients feel fully informed and confident in their decision.

Integrating Objection Handling and Trial Closes

In the final segment of this chapter, we bring together the skills of objection handling and trial closes into a cohesive strategy. Discover how a synchronized approach enhances your ability to navigate objections seamlessly and strategically move towards deal finalization.

Strategic Objection Handling within the Sales Funnel: Understand how objection handling fits into the broader sales funnel. Explore techniques for strategically addressing objections at various stages, ensuring a smooth progression toward deal closure.

Using Trial Closes to Overcome Specific Objections: Tailor trial closes to address specific objections effectively. Learn how trial closes can serve as powerful tools for gaining commitment and alleviating client concerns, ultimately paving the way for successful deal closure.

THE DIGITAL SALES LANDSCAPE

In the ever-evolving realm of sales, the digital landscape has emerged as a transformative force, offering unprecedented opportunities for engagement, outreach, and efficiency. This chapter is dedicated to exploring the intricacies of the digital sales landscape, focusing on leveraging technology for sales excellence and harnessing the power of social media for effective selling.

Leveraging Technology for Sales Excellence

The Technological Revolution in Sales

Technology has revolutionized the sales process, providing tools and platforms that enhance efficiency and effectiveness. This section explores the transformative impact of technology on sales and its role in shaping the modern sales landscape.

Embracing Sales Automation Tools: Delve into the world of sales automation and understand how tools like customer relationship management (CRM) systems, email automation, and artificial intelligence (AI) can streamline processes, enhance productivity, and provide valuable insights.

Data-Driven Decision Making: Explore the power of data in sales decision-making. Understand how analytics and data-driven insights can inform strategies, refine targeting, and optimize the entire sales funnel for greater effectiveness.

Innovative Sales Technologies: Stay abreast of emerging technologies shaping the sales landscape, from chatbots and virtual assistants to predictive analytics. Discover how innovative solutions can elevate your sales approach and offer a competitive edge.

Personalization in the Digital Age

In the digital era, personalization has become a cornerstone of successful sales strategies. This section explores how technology facilitates personalized interactions and enhances the overall customer experience.

Dynamic Personalization Strategies: Explore dynamic personalization techniques that tailor sales messages, content, and recommendations based on individual customer preferences, behavior, and demographics.

Implementing AI-Powered Personalization: Understand the role of artificial intelligence in personalization. Explore how AI algorithms analyze data to predict customer needs, enabling the delivery of personalized recommendations and experiences.

Integrating Social Media for Effective Selling

The Social Selling Paradigm

Social media has transformed the way businesses connect with their audience. This section delves into the concept of social selling and how leveraging social media platforms can enhance your sales efforts.

Understanding Social Selling: Explore the fundamentals of social selling, which involves using social media to identify, connect with, and nurture prospects. Understand how social platforms serve as powerful channels for building relationships and driving sales.

Building a Personal Brand on Social Media: Personal branding is integral to social selling success. Learn how to craft and cultivate a compelling personal brand on social media, establishing credibility and attracting a loyal audience.

Platforms and Strategies for Social Selling

Different social media platforms offer unique opportunities for engagement and outreach. This section examines key platforms and effective strategies for leveraging them in your social selling endeavors.

LinkedIn for B2B Selling: Uncover the potential of LinkedIn as a powerhouse for B2B social selling. Explore strategies for building a professional presence, connecting with decision-makers, and showcasing your expertise.

Twitter for Real-Time Engagement: Understand how Twitter's real-time nature can be harnessed for effective engagement. Learn strategies for using hashtags, participating in relevant conversations, and positioning yourself as an industry thought leader.

Instagram for Visual Storytelling: Explore the visual storytelling capabilities of Instagram. Discover how to use visual content, such as images and videos, to tell compelling stories, showcase products, and engage with your audience in a visually-driven manner.

Facebook for Community Building: Dive into the community-building potential of Facebook. Learn how to create and foster communities, share valuable content, and leverage the platform's advertising features for targeted outreach.

Maximizing the Synergy of Technology and Social Selling

Creating an Integrated Digital Sales Strategy

In the final segment of this chapter, we bring together the concepts of leveraging technology and integrating social selling into a cohesive digital sales strategy. Discover how the synergy of these elements amplifies your sales efforts and positions you for success in the digital era.

Integrating Technology into Social Selling: Explore strategies for seamlessly integrating technology into your social selling initiatives. Learn how to leverage CRM systems, marketing automation, and other tools to enhance the efficiency and effectiveness of your social selling endeavors.

Measuring and Analyzing Digital Sales Performance: Implement metrics to measure the performance of your digital sales strategy.

Understand how to track key performance indicators (KPIs) related to social engagement, lead generation, and conversion rates.

DATA-DRIVEN DECISION MAKING IN SALES

In the dynamic landscape of modern sales, the ability to harness data for informed decision-making is a critical skill that separates successful professionals from the rest. This chapter delves into the realm of data-driven decision-making in sales, exploring how analytics can be used to optimize sales performance and understanding the key metrics that pave the way for success.

Using Analytics to Optimize Sales Performance

The Power of Sales Analytics

Sales analytics is the compass that guides strategic decision-making, offering insights that go beyond intuition. This section explores the transformative impact of analytics on sales performance and how it can be harnessed to optimize every facet of the sales process.

Understanding Sales Analytics: Delve into the fundamentals of sales analytics, which involves the collection, analysis, and interpretation of data to inform sales strategies. Learn how analytics can uncover patterns, trends, and opportunities that lead to more informed decision-making.

Implementing Predictive Analytics: Explore the realm of predictive analytics in sales. Understand how advanced statistical models and machine learning algorithms can forecast future trends, customer behavior, and sales outcomes, enabling proactive strategies.

Tailoring Strategies with Customer Segmentation

Customer segmentation is a cornerstone of personalized and effective sales strategies. This section explores how data-driven insights can inform customer segmentation, allowing for tailored approaches that resonate with diverse audience segments.

Data-Driven Customer Profiling: Explore the process of creating detailed customer profiles based on data-driven insights. Understand how demographic, behavioral, and transactional data can be leveraged to segment customers into distinct groups.

Segment-Specific Sales Strategies: Tailor sales strategies for each customer segment based on their unique characteristics and preferences. Learn how segmentation enables personalized messaging, targeted promotions, and a more engaging customer experience.

Understanding Key Metrics for Success

Identifying Core Sales Metrics

Key performance indicators (KPIs) serve as the heartbeat of a data-driven sales strategy. This section examines essential sales metrics that provide a comprehensive view of performance and guide strategic decision-making.

Sales Revenue and Growth Metrics: Explore metrics related to sales revenue and growth, including total sales, growth rate, and revenue per customer. Understand how these metrics offer insights into overall sales health and sustainability.

Conversion Rates and Sales Funnel Metrics: Dive into conversion rates and metrics related to the sales funnel. Explore the conversion rates at each stage of the funnel, from lead acquisition to deal closure, and identify opportunities for optimization.

Customer Acquisition Cost (CAC) and Lifetime Value (LTV): Understand the balance between the cost of acquiring a customer and the value they bring over their lifetime. Explore how CAC and LTV metrics inform decisions about marketing investments and customer retention strategies.

Performance Metrics for Sales Teams

The effectiveness of sales teams is measured through a range of performance metrics. This section explores key indicators that assess the productivity, efficiency, and success of sales teams.

Sales Pipeline Metrics: Explore metrics related to the sales pipeline, including the number of deals in the pipeline, average deal size, and pipeline velocity. Understand how these metrics provide insights into the health and efficiency of the sales process.

Individual Sales Rep Metrics: Dive into metrics that evaluate the performance of individual sales representatives. Explore measures such as close rates, deal size, and activity levels to identify top performers, areas for improvement, and coaching opportunities.

Implementing Data-Driven Decision Making

Creating a Data-Driven Culture

A successful transition to data-driven decision-making requires a cultural shift within the sales organization. This section explores strategies for fostering a culture that values and leverages data to drive excellence.

Promoting Data Literacy: Understand the importance of data literacy among sales teams. Explore strategies for providing training and resources that empower sales professionals to interpret and utilize data effectively.

Encouraging Experimentation and Iteration: Foster a culture of experimentation and iteration. Learn how encouraging sales teams to test new strategies, measure outcomes, and iterate based on data-driven insights contributes to continuous improvement.

Leveraging Technology for Data-Driven Insights

Technology serves as the backbone of data-driven decision-making in sales. This section explores the tools and technologies that empower sales teams to collect, analyze, and derive actionable insights from data.

Implementing Customer Relationship Management (CRM) Systems: Dive into the role of CRM systems in centralizing customer data and providing a comprehensive view of customer interactions. Explore how CRM systems contribute to data-driven decision-making.

Utilizing Business Intelligence (BI) Tools: Explore the capabilities of business intelligence tools in transforming raw data into actionable insights. Understand how BI tools enable visualization, analysis, and reporting that guide strategic decision-making.

Maximizing the Impact of Data-Driven Decision Making

Creating a Data-Driven Sales Strategy

In the final segment of this chapter, we bring together the principles of data-driven decision-making into a cohesive sales strategy. Discover how a systematic and strategic approach maximizes the impact of data in optimizing sales performance.

Integrating Data into Sales Planning: Explore how data can be integrated into sales planning processes. Understand how insights from historical data, market trends, and customer behaviors inform strategic planning and goal-setting.

Continuous Monitoring and Adjustment: Implement a framework for continuous monitoring and adjustment based on data-driven insights. Learn how to establish feedback loops that allow sales strategies to evolve in response to changing market dynamics.

MASTERING THE ART OF NEGOTIATION

Negotiation is the heartbeat of successful sales, a delicate dance where parties seek mutually beneficial outcomes. This chapter delves into the art of negotiation, unraveling strategies for achieving win-win results and providing guidance on navigating challenging negotiation scenarios with finesse.

Negotiation Strategies for Win-Win Outcomes

The Collaborative Approach to Negotiation

Successful negotiation is not a zero-sum game; it's a collaborative process that aims for mutual gains. This section explores the principles of collaborative negotiation and strategies for achieving win-win outcomes.

Building Rapport and Trust: Establishing a foundation of trust is paramount in negotiation. Explore techniques for building rapport, demonstrating reliability, and fostering an environment of trust that facilitates open communication.

Identifying Shared Interests: Dive into the identification of shared interests between parties. Understand how uncovering common ground allows for the creation of solutions that address both parties' needs, fostering a collaborative negotiating atmosphere.

Creating Value Through Creativity: Explore the concept of value creation in negotiation. Learn how to think creatively, identify additional value that can be exchanged, and craft solutions that exceed the initial expectations of both parties.

Effective Communication Strategies in Negotiation

Communication is the bedrock of negotiation, influencing perceptions and outcomes. This section delves into advanced communication strategies that enhance your ability to convey messages, understand counterparts, and navigate negotiations successfully.

Active Listening and Empathetic Communication: Master the art of active listening in negotiation. Understand how empathetic communication, combined with reflective listening, allows you to comprehend the motivations and concerns of the other party.

Strategic Use of Verbal and Non-Verbal Cues: Explore the strategic use of verbal and non-verbal cues in negotiation. Learn how tone, body language, and choice of words contribute to effective communication and influence the dynamics of the negotiation process.

Crafting Persuasive Arguments: Hone your ability to craft persuasive arguments that resonate with the other party. Explore techniques for presenting your case clearly, highlighting benefits, and addressing concerns to build a compelling narrative.

Handling Difficult Negotiation Scenarios

Navigating Common Challenges in Negotiation

Negotiation often presents challenges that require adept handling. This section explores common obstacles in negotiation scenarios and provides strategies for overcoming them.

Dealing with Resistance and Objections: Explore techniques for handling resistance and objections in negotiation. Learn how to address concerns effectively, reframe objections as opportunities, and guide the negotiation toward a positive resolution.

Managing Competitive and Aggressive Tactics: Delve into strategies for managing competitive and aggressive negotiation tactics. Understand how to maintain composure, set boundaries, and redirect the negotiation toward a more collaborative path.

Breaking Deadlocks and Stalemates: Navigate deadlocks and stalemates with strategic interventions. Explore techniques for breaking impasses, introducing new perspectives, and finding creative solutions to revitalize negotiations.

Adapting to Cultural and Personality Differences

Negotiations often involve parties with diverse cultural backgrounds and personalities. This section explores how to adapt your negotiation approach to bridge cultural gaps and navigate diverse personalities effectively.

Cultural Sensitivity in Negotiation: Understand the importance of cultural sensitivity in negotiation. Explore strategies for recognizing and respecting cultural differences, adapting communication styles, and building trust across diverse contexts.

Navigating Different Personality Types: Dive into techniques for navigating negotiations with different personality types. From assertive and competitive negotiators to those who prefer collaboration, learn how to tailor your approach for optimal outcomes.

Integrating Strategies for Success in Negotiation

Crafting a Comprehensive Negotiation Strategy

In the final segment of this chapter, we bring together the negotiation strategies for win-win outcomes and handling difficult scenarios into a comprehensive approach. Discover how a strategic blend of collaborative techniques and adept handling of challenges positions you as a masterful negotiator.

Creating a Negotiation Plan: Develop a negotiation plan that encompasses your goals, strategies, and potential challenges. Learn how careful preparation allows you to enter negotiations with clarity, confidence, and flexibility.

Adapting Strategies Throughout the Process: Understand the dynamic nature of negotiations and the importance of adapting strategies throughout the process. Explore how ongoing assessment and strategic adjustments contribute to successful negotiation outcomes.

Evaluating and Learning from Each Negotiation: Implement a framework for evaluating and learning from each negotiation. Understand how reflection and feedback contribute to your growth as a negotiator, refining your skills and strategies over time.

ADAPTING TO CHANGING MARKET DYNAMICS

In the fast-paced landscape of business, the ability to adapt to changing market dynamics is a hallmark of successful sales professionals. This chapter explores the imperative of staying agile in a dynamic business environment and provides insights into innovating your sales approach for modern markets.

Staying Agile in a Dynamic Business Environment

Understanding Market Dynamics

Market dynamics are the forces that impact the behavior of buyers, sellers, and competitors within an industry. This section explores the factors that contribute to changing market dynamics and the importance of staying attuned to these shifts.

Market Trends and Shifts: Dive into the identification of market trends and shifts. Understand how changes in customer preferences, emerging technologies, and external factors such as economic conditions influence the dynamics of the business environment.

Competitor Analysis and Benchmarking: Explore the role of competitor analysis in understanding market dynamics. Learn how benchmarking against industry competitors provides insights into best practices, potential gaps, and opportunities for differentiation.

The Agile Mindset in Sales

Agility in sales involves the ability to respond swiftly and effectively to changing circumstances. This section delves into the agile mindset and strategies for cultivating adaptability in sales teams.

Cultivating a Growth Mindset: Foster a growth mindset within your sales team. Understand how viewing challenges as opportunities for learning and improvement contributes to a culture of continuous adaptation and innovation.

Agile Decision-Making Processes: Explore agile decision-making processes that allow for quick, informed choices. Learn how streamlined decision-making, empowered teams, and data-driven insights contribute to adaptive responses in dynamic environments.

Flexibility in Sales Strategies: Embrace flexibility in sales strategies. Explore how a flexible approach allows sales professionals to pivot, experiment, and iterate based on evolving market dynamics and customer needs.

Innovating Your Sales Approach for Modern Markets

Embracing Technological Advancements

Innovation in sales is closely tied to leveraging technological advancements to enhance processes and customer experiences. This section explores how adopting cutting-edge technologies can transform your sales approach.

Implementing Sales Automation and AI: Delve into the implementation of sales automation tools and artificial intelligence (AI) in your sales processes. Understand how these technologies streamline workflows, enhance personalization, and provide actionable insights.

Utilizing Predictive Analytics: Explore the potential of predictive analytics in sales. Understand how predictive models can forecast trends, identify potential leads, and guide strategic decision-making in a forward-looking manner.

Personalization and Customer-Centricity

In modern markets, customers expect personalized and tailored experiences. This section explores strategies for infusing personalization and customer-centricity into your sales approach.

Dynamic Personalization Strategies: Build on the concept of dynamic personalization discussed in Chapter 8. Explore advanced strategies for tailoring your messaging, content, and interactions based on real-time customer behaviors and preferences.

Customer Journey Mapping: Dive into customer journey mapping as a tool for understanding and enhancing the customer experience. Learn how mapping the customer journey identifies touchpoints, pain points, and opportunities for personalized engagement.

Navigating the Integration of Sales Technologies

Creating a Seamless Tech Ecosystem

The integration of sales technologies is critical for optimizing performance and adapting to modern market demands. This section explores how to create a seamless tech ecosystem that maximizes the benefits of integrated technologies.

Integrating CRM, Marketing Automation, and Sales Tools: Dive into the integration of customer relationship management (CRM), marketing automation, and other sales tools. Understand how a cohesive tech ecosystem enhances collaboration, data sharing, and overall efficiency.

Data Security and Compliance: Explore considerations for data security and compliance in an integrated tech environment. Learn how to safeguard sensitive information, comply with regulations, and build trust with customers regarding data protection.

Embracing a Culture of Innovation and Continuous Improvement

Fostering a Culture of Innovation

Innovation is not just about technology; it's a mindset that permeates an organization. This section explores strategies for fostering a culture of innovation and continuous improvement within your sales team.

Encouraging Idea Generation and Collaboration: Explore techniques for encouraging idea generation and collaboration within your sales team. Understand how cross-functional collaboration and diverse perspectives contribute to innovative solutions.

Implementing Feedback Loops: Dive into the importance of feedback loops in driving continuous improvement. Learn how implementing regular feedback mechanisms allows for the identification of areas for enhancement and refinement of strategies.

Adapting Sales Strategies to External Factors

Navigating Economic Changes and Global Trends

External factors, such as economic changes and global trends, have a profound impact on market dynamics. This section explores strategies for navigating external factors and adapting sales strategies accordingly.

Scenario Planning for Economic Changes: Delve into the concept of scenario planning for economic changes. Understand how anticipating and preparing for various economic scenarios allows your sales team to adapt strategies proactively.

Globalization and Cultural Intelligence: Explore the impact of globalization on sales and the importance of cultural intelligence. Learn how understanding diverse cultural contexts and adapting sales approaches accordingly fosters successful international engagements.

Maximizing Adaptive Leadership in Sales

Leading Through Change

Adaptive leadership is crucial for guiding sales teams through periods of change and uncertainty. This section explores the principles of adaptive leadership and strategies for leading effectively in dynamic business environments.

Communicating a Compelling Vision: Dive into the role of visionary leadership in times of change. Understand how communicating a compelling vision inspires confidence, fosters alignment, and motivates your sales team to adapt and excel.

Empowering and Supporting Teams: Explore strategies for empowering and supporting your sales teams during transitions. Learn how providing autonomy, fostering a sense of belonging, and offering resources for skill development contribute to resilience and success.

Agile Coaching and Training: Implement agile coaching and training practices. Understand how ongoing coaching and training that align with agile principles enable your sales team to continuously learn, adapt, and thrive in changing market dynamics.

Navigating Uncertainty with Confidence

Strategies for Future-Proofing Sales

In the final segment of this chapter, we bring together the strategies for staying agile and innovating your sales approach into a holistic approach for future-proofing sales. Discover how a proactive and adaptive mindset positions your sales team to navigate uncertainty with confidence.

Developing a Future-Ready Sales Strategy: Explore the principles of future-ready sales strategies. Learn how a strategic blend of agility, innovation, and adaptive leadership creates a resilient and future-proof sales approach.

Anticipating and Embracing Change: Understand the importance of anticipating and embracing change as an integral part of the business landscape. Explore how cultivating a mindset that sees change as an opportunity rather than a challenge contributes to sustained success.

Measuring and Adjusting for Long-Term Success: Implement metrics for measuring the long-term success of your adaptive strategies. Learn how to assess the impact of agility and innovation on sales performance, customer satisfaction, and overall organizational resilience.

BUILDING A PERSONAL BRAND FOR SALES PROFESSIONALS

In the competitive realm of sales, building a compelling personal brand is a powerful strategy for establishing credibility, fostering trust, and differentiating yourself in the minds of clients. This chapter explores the art of creating an authentic and memorable sales persona and delves into how personal branding can be leveraged for sales success.

Creating an Authentic and Memorable Sales Persona

Defining Your Unique Selling Proposition (USP)

Your Unique Selling Proposition (USP) is the foundation of your personal brand. This section explores the process of defining your USP and how it sets the stage for creating an authentic and memorable sales persona.

Identifying Your Core Strengths and Expertise: Delve into self-assessment to identify your core strengths and areas of expertise. Understand how aligning your skills with your passion and the needs of your target audience forms the basis of your unique selling proposition.

Crafting a Distinctive Value Proposition: Explore the art of crafting a distinctive value proposition that communicates the unique value you bring to clients. Learn how to articulate your USP in a clear and compelling manner that resonates with your target audience.

Authenticity in Sales: Building Genuine Connections

Authenticity is the cornerstone of a memorable sales persona. This section delves into the importance of authenticity and strategies for building genuine connections with clients.

Aligning Your Values with Your Brand: Explore the alignment of your personal values with your brand. Understand how showcasing your authentic self, values, and beliefs creates a genuine and relatable connection with clients.

Storytelling as a Tool for Authenticity: Dive into the art of storytelling as a powerful tool for conveying authenticity. Learn how sharing personal stories, challenges, and triumphs creates a narrative that humanizes your brand and fosters connection.

Developing a Consistent Brand Image

Consistency is key to building a recognizable and memorable brand. This section explores strategies for developing a consistent brand image across various touchpoints.

Creating a Cohesive Visual Identity: Delve into the visual elements of your brand, including logo, color palette, and imagery. Understand how a cohesive visual identity enhances brand recognition and reinforces the consistency of your personal brand.

Consistent Messaging and Tone of Voice: Explore the importance of consistent messaging and tone of voice in your communications. Learn how maintaining a consistent brand voice across written and verbal communication reinforces the authenticity and reliability of your sales persona.

Leveraging Personal Branding for Sales Success

Establishing Online Presence and Visibility

In the digital age, an online presence is a crucial component of personal branding. This section explores strategies for establishing a strong online presence and increasing visibility.

Optimizing Your LinkedIn Profile: Dive into the optimization of your LinkedIn profile, a key platform for professional networking. Learn how to create a compelling headline, craft a engaging summary, and showcase your achievements to enhance your online presence.

Creating and Curating Content: Explore the creation and curation of content to demonstrate your expertise. Understand how sharing valuable insights, industry trends, and thought leadership content positions you as an authority in your field and boosts online visibility.

Networking and Building Relationships

Personal branding is not just about visibility; it's also about building meaningful relationships. This section delves into strategies for networking and fostering connections that contribute to sales success.

Strategic Networking and Relationship Building:
Explore the principles of strategic networking for
sales professionals. Learn how to identify and
connect with key influencers, clients, and industry
peers to expand your network and open doors to
new opportunities.

Building Trust Through Consistent Engagement:
Delve into the importance of consistent
engagement in building trust. Understand how
active participation in online forums, industry
events, and client interactions contributes to the
trustworthiness of your personal brand.

*Showcasing Expertise Through Thought
Leadership*

Positioning yourself as a thought leader in your
industry is a powerful way to leverage personal
branding for sales success. This section explores
strategies for showcasing your expertise through
thought leadership.

*Creating and Publishing Thought Leadership
Content*: Explore the creation and publishing of
thought leadership content. Learn how to write
articles, whitepapers, or blog posts that
demonstrate your expertise, contribute valuable

insights, and position you as a thought leader in your domain.

Speaking Engagements and Webinars: Delve into the opportunities presented by speaking engagements and webinars. Understand how presenting your knowledge and insights to a wider audience enhances your credibility, expands your reach, and establishes you as an authority in your field.

Measuring the Impact of Your Personal Brand

Key Performance Indicators (KPIs) for Personal Branding

Effective personal branding is measurable. This section explores key performance indicators (KPIs) that help gauge the impact of your personal brand on sales success.

Quantitative Metrics: Analyzing Reach and Engagement: Dive into quantitative metrics such as reach and engagement on online platforms. Understand how analyzing the number of connections, followers, likes, comments, and shares provides insights into the impact of your personal brand.

Qualitative Metrics: Assessing Reputation and Client Feedback: Explore qualitative metrics that assess your reputation and client feedback. Understand how testimonials, reviews, and client endorsements contribute to building a positive reputation and validate the effectiveness of your personal brand.

Iterating and Evolving Your Personal Brand

Personal branding is not static; it evolves with time and experiences. This section explores the importance of iteration and continuous improvement in your personal brand.

Feedback Loops and Self-Reflection: Delve into the concept of feedback loops and self-reflection. Learn how seeking feedback from peers, mentors, and clients, coupled with regular self-reflection, allows you to identify areas for improvement and refine your personal brand over time.

Adapting to Changing Industry Trends: Explore strategies for adapting your personal brand to changing industry trends. Understand how staying attuned to shifts in your industry and adjusting your brand accordingly ensures relevance and continued success.

Sustaining Sales Success Through Your Personal Brand

Building Long-Term Client Relationships

Your personal brand plays a pivotal role in building and sustaining long-term client relationships. This section explores strategies for leveraging your personal brand to foster client loyalty.

Consistent Communication and Follow-Up: Dive into the importance of consistent communication and follow-up in client relationships. Learn how maintaining regular contact, providing updates, and expressing genuine interest contribute to the longevity of client relationships.

Client-Centric Approach in Sales: Explore the principles of a client-centric approach in sales. Understand how aligning your personal brand with a focus on solving client problems, delivering value, and exceeding expectations creates a positive and enduring impression.

Mentorship and Giving Back

Mentorship and giving back are integral components of a holistic personal brand. This section explores the benefits of mentorship, both as a mentor and a mentee, and the impact of giving back to the community.

Engaging in Mentorship: Delve into the rewards of engaging in mentorship. Learn how serving as a mentor or seeking mentorship enhances your personal brand, contributes to professional development, and fosters a sense of community within your industry.

Contributing to the Community and Industry: Explore the impact of contributing to the community and industry. Understand how volunteering, participating in industry events, and sharing knowledge with others not only enriches your personal brand but also contributes to the collective success of your professional ecosystem.

Navigating Challenges in Personal Branding for Sales Professionals

Overcoming Common Challenges

Building a personal brand is not without challenges. This section explores common challenges faced by sales professionals in personal branding and strategies for overcoming them.

Authenticity Amidst Professionalism: Delve into the challenge of maintaining authenticity while upholding professionalism. Learn how to strike a balance that aligns with your personality, resonates with your audience, and meets the expectations of a professional sales environment.

Managing Negative Feedback and Criticism: Explore strategies for managing negative feedback and criticism. Understand how turning criticism into constructive insights, responding with grace, and using feedback as a catalyst for improvement contribute to the resilience of your personal brand.

Integrating Personal Branding into Sales Culture

Fostering a Personal Branding Culture

In the final segment of this chapter, we bring together the strategies for building a personal brand, leveraging it for sales success, and navigating challenges into a comprehensive approach for fostering a personal branding culture within sales teams.

Cultivating Personal Brands Within the Team: Explore strategies for cultivating personal brands within your sales team. Learn how fostering a culture that values individuality, encourages personal brand development, and recognizes diverse strengths contributes to collective success.

Aligning Personal Brands with Organizational Values: Understand the importance of aligning personal brands with organizational values. Explore how individual personal brands, when aligned with the overarching values and goals of the organization, create a cohesive and impactful sales culture.

SALES LEADERSHIP AND TEAM MANAGEMENT

Effective sales leadership is the linchpin of success in the dynamic world of sales. This chapter explores the art of leading high-performing sales teams and the strategies for motivating and inspiring sales professionals to achieve exceptional results.

Leading High-Performing Sales Teams

Defining the Vision and Mission

Sales leadership begins with a clear vision and mission that guides the team toward a common goal. This section explores the process of defining a compelling vision and mission for a high-performing sales team.

Crafting a Vision for Sales Success: Dive into the crafting of a vision that inspires and motivates the sales team. Understand how a compelling vision creates a sense of purpose, aligns team members, and sets the foundation for achieving collective goals.

Defining a Mission Statement: Explore the development of a mission statement that encapsulates the team's purpose and values. Learn how a well-defined mission statement serves as a guiding beacon, informing decision-making and fostering a shared sense of identity within the team.

Building a Culture of Collaboration and Accountability

A positive team culture is essential for high performance. This section delves into strategies for building a culture of collaboration and accountability within a sales team.

Fostering Open Communication: Explore the importance of open communication in a sales team. Learn how creating an environment where team members feel heard, valued, and encouraged to share ideas contributes to a culture of collaboration.

Establishing Accountability Structures: Dive into the establishment of accountability structures that promote individual and collective responsibility. Understand how setting clear expectations, defining roles, and implementing performance metrics foster accountability and drive results.

Developing and Nurturing Talent

Sales leadership involves developing the skills and talents of team members. This section explores strategies for identifying, developing, and nurturing talent within a sales team.

Talent Identification and Recruitment: Delve into the process of talent identification and recruitment. Learn how to recognize the skills, qualities, and potential of individuals that align with the team's objectives, and explore effective recruitment strategies.

Continuous Learning and Development Programs: Explore the implementation of continuous learning and development programs. Understand how ongoing training, mentorship, and skill-building opportunities contribute to the professional growth of team members and enhance overall team performance.

Motivating and Inspiring Sales Professionals

Understanding Motivational Drivers

Motivation is a key factor in sales success. This section explores the various motivational drivers and how sales leaders can understand and leverage them effectively.

Intrinsic and Extrinsic Motivators: Dive into the distinction between intrinsic and extrinsic motivators. Understand how aligning individual motivators, whether internal satisfaction or external rewards, contributes to a well-rounded motivational strategy.

Recognizing and Acknowledging Achievements: Explore the impact of recognizing and acknowledging achievements. Learn how celebrating milestones, accomplishments, and exceptional performance reinforces positive behavior and motivates sales professionals.

Tailoring Motivational Strategies

Motivational strategies should be tailored to the unique needs of individual team members. This section explores the importance of customization in motivational approaches.

Individualized Goal Setting: Delve into the practice of individualized goal setting. Understand how setting personalized, achievable goals for each team member aligns with their aspirations, fosters a sense of ownership, and enhances motivation.

Flexible Incentive Structures: Explore the implementation of flexible incentive structures.

Learn how providing a range of incentives, such as monetary rewards, recognition, and career development opportunities, caters to diverse motivational preferences within the team.

Creating a Positive and Inclusive Work Environment

A positive and inclusive work environment is a cornerstone of motivation and inspiration. This section explores strategies for creating a workplace culture that energizes and uplifts sales professionals.

Promoting a Positive Culture of Recognition: Dive into the promotion of a positive culture of recognition. Learn how acknowledging and appreciating the efforts of team members, both publicly and privately, contributes to a sense of value and belonging.

Fostering Inclusivity and Diversity: Explore the importance of fostering inclusivity and diversity within the sales team. Understand how a diverse and inclusive environment enhances creativity, collaboration, and motivation among team members.

Effective Communication and Leadership Presence

Communication is a powerful tool for motivating and inspiring teams. This section delves into effective communication strategies and the importance of leadership presence.

Transparent and Authentic Communication: Explore the principles of transparent and authentic communication. Learn how openly sharing information, addressing challenges, and expressing vulnerability fosters trust and strengthens the leader-follower relationship.

Building a Leadership Presence: Dive into the concept of leadership presence. Understand how cultivating a strong leadership presence involves projecting confidence, charisma, and a clear sense of purpose that inspires confidence and trust among team members.

Navigating Challenges in Sales Leadership

Overcoming Common Leadership Challenges

Sales leadership is not without its challenges. This section explores common challenges faced by sales leaders and strategies for overcoming them.

Balancing Results and Relationship Building: Delve into the challenge of balancing the pursuit of results with relationship building. Learn how striking a balance between achieving targets and fostering meaningful connections contributes to sustained success.

Handling Conflict and Resolving Disputes: Explore strategies for handling conflict and resolving disputes within the team. Understand how effective conflict resolution techniques, such as active listening and mediation, contribute to a harmonious and productive work environment.

Sustaining High Performance and Continuous Improvement

Establishing a Culture of Continuous Improvement

Sustaining high performance requires a commitment to continuous improvement. This section explores strategies for establishing a culture of continuous learning and growth within a sales team.

Encouraging Feedback and Iteration: Delve into the importance of encouraging feedback and iteration. Learn how creating channels for open feedback, both upward and downward, facilitates continuous improvement and adaptation to changing circumstances.

Implementing Data-Driven Decision Making: Explore the integration of data-driven decision-making in sales leadership. Understand how leveraging analytics and key performance indicators (KPIs) informs strategic decisions, identifies areas for improvement, and enhances overall team performance.

Team Celebrations and Recognition Programs

Celebrating achievements and recognizing exceptional performance is a vital component of sustaining high performance. This section explores the implementation of team celebrations and recognition programs.

Organizing Team-Building Events: Dive into the organization of team-building events. Learn how fostering camaraderie, collaboration, and a sense of shared success through team celebrations contributes to a positive and motivated work environment.

Structured Recognition Programs: Explore the implementation of structured recognition programs. Understand how formal recognition programs, such as "Salesperson of the Month" or "Top Performer Awards," provide tangible acknowledgment of outstanding contributions.

Strategic Planning for Long-Term Success

In the final segment of this chapter, we bring together the strategies for leading high-performing sales teams, motivating and inspiring sales professionals, navigating challenges, and sustaining high performance into a comprehensive approach for strategic planning and long-term success.

Setting Long-Term Goals and Objectives: Explore the process of setting long-term goals and objectives for the sales team. Learn how aligning the team's aspirations with overarching organizational goals creates a roadmap for sustained success.

Adapting Strategies to Industry Trends: Delve into the importance of adapting strategies to industry trends. Understand how staying attuned to shifts in the market, emerging technologies, and customer behaviors allows sales leaders to lead their teams with agility and foresight.

Empowering Sales Professionals for Autonomy: Explore the empowerment of sales professionals for autonomy and decision-making. Learn how fostering a culture that empowers individuals to take initiative, make informed decisions, and contribute to the strategic direction of the team enhances overall team effectiveness.

HARNESSING THE POWER OF STORYTELLING IN SALES

Storytelling is a potent tool in the arsenal of sales professionals, enabling them to engage customers, convey value, and establish emotional connections. This chapter explores the art of crafting compelling sales narratives and how to use stories to connect with customers on an emotional level.

Crafting Compelling Sales Narratives

Understanding the Psychology of Storytelling

The psychology of storytelling plays a pivotal role in capturing the attention and interest of customers. This section explores the fundamental principles of storytelling psychology and its application in sales.

Emotional Resonance and Memory: Delve into the impact of emotional resonance on memory retention. Understand how stories that evoke emotions create lasting impressions, making your sales message more memorable and compelling.

The Power of Relatability: Explore the concept of relatability in storytelling. Learn how crafting narratives that resonate with the experiences, challenges, and aspirations of your audience fosters a sense of connection and understanding.

Identifying Key Elements of a Sales Narrative

A well-crafted sales narrative comprises key elements that captivate the audience and drive the sales message. This section explores the essential components of a compelling sales narrative.

Introduction: Setting the Stage: Dive into the importance of a captivating introduction. Learn how to set the stage for your narrative, grabbing the attention of your audience from the outset and creating curiosity.

Conflict and Resolution: Explore the role of conflict and resolution in sales narratives. Understand how introducing challenges or obstacles, followed by the resolution through your product or service, adds tension and interest to your story.

Customer Success Stories and Testimonials: Delve into the incorporation of customer success stories and testimonials. Learn how featuring real-life examples of how your product or service benefited customers adds credibility and authenticity to your narrative.

Using Stories to Connect with Customers Emotionally

Building Emotional Bridges with Customers

Emotional connections are the cornerstone of successful sales relationships. This section explores strategies for building emotional bridges with customers through storytelling.

Empathy in Storytelling: Explore the role of empathy in crafting stories. Learn how understanding and acknowledging the emotions of your customers allows you to tailor narratives that resonate with their needs and concerns.

Showcasing Authenticity: Dive into the importance of authenticity in storytelling. Understand how being genuine and transparent in your narratives builds trust and authenticity, creating a stronger emotional connection with customers.

Tailoring Stories to Different Customer Personas

Different customers have varied preferences and motivations. This section explores the art of tailoring stories to different customer personas to maximize impact.

Segmenting Your Audience: Delve into the segmentation of your audience based on personas. Learn how identifying distinct customer personas allows you to customize stories that address the unique needs, preferences, and pain points of each segment.

Adapting Tone and Style: Explore the adaptation of tone and style to align with different customer personas. Understand how adjusting the narrative tone, language, and style enhances relatability and resonates more effectively with diverse audiences.

Leveraging Visual and Multimedia Elements

The integration of visual and multimedia elements enhances the storytelling experience. This section explores how visuals can complement and reinforce your sales narratives.

Utilizing Engaging Visuals: Delve into the use of engaging visuals, such as images, infographics, and videos, in your sales narratives. Learn how visual elements capture attention, convey information effectively, and amplify the emotional impact of your stories.

Interactive Storytelling Formats: Explore the potential of interactive storytelling formats. Understand how incorporating interactive elements, such as quizzes, surveys, or augmented reality, engages customers on a deeper level and creates a memorable experience.

Storytelling Across Different Sales Channels

Storytelling is a versatile tool that can be applied across various sales channels. This section explores how to adapt and deploy storytelling effectively in diverse sales environments.

Storytelling in In-Person Sales Presentations: Delve into the nuances of storytelling in in-person sales presentations. Learn how to use body language, vocal tone, and interactive elements to enhance the impact of your narratives during face-to-face interactions.

Adapting Stories for Online Platforms: Explore strategies for adapting stories for online platforms, including websites, social media, and email. Understand how to leverage the unique features of each platform to deliver compelling narratives to a broader audience.

Measuring the Impact of Sales Storytelling

Key Performance Indicators (KPIs) for Sales Storytelling

Effective sales storytelling is measurable. This section explores key performance indicators (KPIs) that help gauge the impact of your storytelling efforts.

Customer Engagement Metrics: Dive into customer engagement metrics, including time spent on pages, click-through rates, and social media interactions. Learn how analyzing these metrics provides insights into the level of customer engagement with your storytelling content.

Conversion Rates and Sales Metrics: Explore the correlation between storytelling and conversion rates. Understand how tracking conversion metrics, such as lead conversion rates and sales closures, allows you to assess the direct impact of storytelling on sales outcomes.

Iterating and Evolving Your Storytelling Strategy

Storytelling is a dynamic practice that benefits from iteration and continuous improvement. This section explores the importance of refining and evolving your storytelling strategy over time.

Gathering Feedback from Customers: Delve into the practice of gathering feedback from customers about your storytelling efforts. Learn how customer feedback provides valuable insights into the effectiveness of your narratives and areas for improvement.

Adapting Stories Based on Performance: Explore the iterative process of adapting stories based on performance data. Understand how analyzing KPIs and customer feedback informs strategic adjustments, allowing you to refine your storytelling strategy for optimal impact.

Navigating Challenges in Sales Storytelling

Overcoming Common Storytelling Challenges

Storytelling in sales is not without its challenges. This section explores common challenges faced by sales professionals in storytelling and strategies for overcoming them.

Balancing Emotion and Information: Delve into the challenge of balancing emotion and information in storytelling. Learn how to strike a harmonious balance, ensuring that your narratives are emotionally resonant while conveying essential product or service information.

Tailoring Stories for Complex Products or Services: Explore strategies for tailoring stories for complex products or services. Understand how to simplify complex concepts, highlight key benefits, and create narratives that demystify intricacies for customers.

Integrating Storytelling into Sales Culture

Fostering a Storytelling Culture within Sales Teams

In the final segment of this chapter, we bring together the strategies for crafting compelling sales narratives, using stories to connect with customers emotionally, measuring impact, and overcoming challenges into a comprehensive approach for fostering a storytelling culture within sales teams.

Cultivating a Culture of Storytelling: Explore strategies for cultivating a culture of storytelling within your sales team. Learn how encouraging team members to share success stories, providing training on effective storytelling techniques, and creating platforms for storytelling exchanges contribute to a vibrant storytelling culture.

Aligning Stories with Brand Values: Understand the importance of aligning stories with brand values. Explore how ensuring consistency between the narratives shared by individual team members and the overarching values of the brand creates a cohesive and impactful storytelling culture.

SALES ETHICS AND INTEGRITY

In the complex landscape of sales, ethics and integrity are the cornerstones that not only guide individual actions but also shape the reputation of an entire industry. This chapter delves into the importance of maintaining ethical standards in sales and building a reputation for trustworthiness.

Maintaining Ethical Standards in Sales

Understanding the Foundations of Sales Ethics

Sales ethics are grounded in principles that prioritize honesty, transparency, and fair practices. This section explores the foundational elements of sales ethics.

Honesty and Truthfulness: Delve into the significance of honesty in sales. Learn how transparent and truthful communication fosters trust with customers and establishes a foundation for ethical conduct.

Integrity in Commitments: Explore the role of integrity in fulfilling commitments. Understand how keeping promises and delivering on commitments, whether related to product quality, timelines, or service, reinforces ethical behavior.

Recognizing and Avoiding Unethical Practices

Sales professionals encounter ethical dilemmas in various forms. This section explores common unethical practices in sales and strategies for recognizing and avoiding them.

Pressure Selling and Manipulative Tactics: Delve into the negative impact of pressure selling and manipulative tactics. Learn how avoiding undue pressure and focusing on customer needs promotes ethical sales practices.

Deceptive Marketing and False Claims: Explore the consequences of deceptive marketing and false claims. Understand how transparent communication and accurate representation of products or services are integral to maintaining ethical standards.

Ethical Considerations in Customer Relationships

Building and maintaining ethical customer relationships is essential for long-term success.

This section explores ethical considerations in customer interactions.

Respecting Customer Choices and Boundaries: Delve into the importance of respecting customer choices and boundaries. Learn how understanding and acknowledging the autonomy of customers in decision-making contributes to ethical behavior.

Handling Confidential Information: Explore the ethical handling of confidential customer information. Understand the importance of safeguarding customer data and respecting privacy as a fundamental aspect of ethical conduct.

Building a Reputation for Trustworthiness

The Link Between Ethics and Trust

Trust is the bedrock upon which successful sales relationships are built. This section explores the interconnectedness of ethics and trust in sales.

Trust as a Competitive Advantage: Delve into the concept of trust as a competitive advantage. Learn how a reputation for ethical conduct distinguishes a sales professional or organization and creates a positive perception in the eyes of customers.

Long-Term Relationship Building: Explore the role of ethics in fostering long-term relationships with customers. Understand how consistent ethical behavior contributes to customer loyalty, repeat business, and positive word-of-mouth referrals.

Transparency in Sales Processes

Transparency is a key element in establishing trust with customers. This section explores strategies for integrating transparency into sales processes.

Clear Communication of Terms and Conditions: Delve into the importance of clear communication regarding terms and conditions. Learn how ensuring customers fully understand contractual obligations and commitments contributes to transparency.

Openness About Pricing and Costs: Explore the ethical disclosure of pricing and costs. Understand how transparent pricing practices, without hidden fees or unexpected charges, enhance trust and credibility.

Ethical Considerations in Sales Negotiations

Negotiations are a critical phase where ethical considerations come to the forefront. This section explores ethical conduct during sales negotiations.

Fair and Honest Negotiation Practices: Delve into fair and honest negotiation practices. Learn how avoiding deceptive tactics, being open about options, and seeking mutually beneficial outcomes contribute to ethical negotiations.

Respecting Competitive Dynamics: Explore the ethical treatment of competitors during negotiations. Understand how maintaining respect for competitors and avoiding disparagement contribute to a positive industry image.

Handling Ethical Dilemmas in Sales

Sales professionals often face ethical dilemmas requiring thoughtful consideration. This section explores strategies for identifying, analyzing, and resolving ethical dilemmas.

Ethical Decision-Making Frameworks: Delve into ethical decision-making frameworks. Learn how adopting structured approaches, such as considering consequences, consulting ethical guidelines, and seeking advice, can guide professionals in resolving ethical dilemmas.

Consulting Ethical Guidelines and Codes: Explore the role of industry-specific ethical guidelines and codes. Understand how adherence to established ethical standards within the sales profession provides a framework for decision-making.

Measuring and Demonstrating Ethical Conduct

Key Performance Indicators (KPIs) for Sales Ethics

Measuring and demonstrating ethical conduct require specific indicators. This section explores key performance indicators (KPIs) that gauge the effectiveness of ethical practices in sales.

Customer Satisfaction and Loyalty: Delve into the correlation between customer satisfaction, loyalty, and ethical conduct. Learn how satisfied customers who perceive ethical behavior are more likely to become loyal advocates for a brand.

Number of Ethical Violations Reported: Explore the reporting and tracking of ethical violations. Understand how monitoring the number of reported violations provides insights into the prevalence and nature of ethical challenges within a sales organization.

Building a Culture of Ethics within Sales Teams

Incorporating ethics into the culture of sales teams is instrumental in fostering ethical behavior. This section explores strategies for building a culture of ethics within sales teams.

Ethics Training and Education Programs: Delve into the implementation of ethics training and education programs. Learn how providing resources, training sessions, and ongoing education reinforces ethical behavior and awareness within the team.

Leadership Demonstration of Ethical Values: Explore the role of leadership in demonstrating ethical values. Understand how leaders who embody ethical behavior set a powerful example for team members and contribute to the establishment of a strong ethical culture.

External Certification and Recognition

External certification and recognition validate a commitment to ethical conduct. This section explores certifications and recognition programs related to sales ethics.

Certifications in Sales Ethics: Delve into certifications available in the field of sales ethics. Learn how obtaining certifications, such as those provided by professional organizations or industry bodies, communicates a commitment to ethical standards.

Industry Awards for Ethical Practices: Explore industry awards that recognize ethical practices. Understand how participating in and receiving awards for ethical conduct enhances the reputation of sales professionals and organizations.

Navigating Challenges in Sales Ethics

Overcoming Common Ethical Challenges

Sales professionals encounter specific challenges in maintaining ethical standards. This section explores common challenges and strategies for overcoming them.

Balancing Sales Targets and Ethical Conduct: Delve into the challenge of balancing sales targets and ethical conduct. Learn how aligning sales goals with ethical principles, rather than compromising integrity for short-term gains, contributes to sustainable success.

Addressing Ethical Violations and Misconduct: Explore strategies for addressing ethical violations and misconduct. Understand how prompt and transparent responses, coupled with corrective actions and preventive measures, mitigate the impact of ethical breaches.

Sustaining Ethical Excellence in Sales

Integrating Ethics into Organizational Values

Sustaining ethical excellence requires a holistic approach that integrates ethics into the core values of an organization. This section explores strategies for aligning ethics with organizational values.

Alignment with Organizational Mission and Values: Delve into the alignment of sales ethics with the broader mission and values of the organization. Learn how a cohesive alignment fosters a unified commitment to ethical conduct throughout the entire organization.

Integration into Performance Evaluation: Explore the integration of ethical considerations into performance evaluation. Understand how evaluating sales professionals based on ethical behavior reinforces the importance of ethics in achieving organizational goals.

Periodic Ethics Audits and Reviews

Periodic audits and reviews are essential to assess and enhance ethical practices. This section explores the implementation of ethics audits within sales teams.

Assessing Adherence to Ethical Guidelines: Delve into the assessment of adherence to ethical guidelines through audits. Learn how periodic reviews identify areas for improvement, verify compliance, and provide valuable insights for refining ethical practices.

Continuous Improvement Initiatives: Explore the integration of continuous improvement initiatives based on audit findings. Understand how using audit results as a foundation for ongoing improvement contributes to sustained ethical excellence.

Stakeholder Engagement in Ethical Practices

Engaging stakeholders in ethical practices strengthens the collective commitment to ethical conduct. This section explores strategies for involving various stakeholders in the ethical framework of sales.

Customer Feedback on Ethical Practices: Delve into the collection of customer feedback on ethical practices. Learn how actively seeking and incorporating customer perspectives contributes to refining and reinforcing ethical standards.

Collaboration with Industry Partners: Explore collaborative initiatives with industry partners to promote ethical practices. Understand how alliances and partnerships focused on ethical conduct create a shared commitment to raising ethical standards across the industry.

CONTINUOUS LEARNING AND PROFESSIONAL DEVELOPMENT

In the dynamic landscape of sales, continuous learning and professional development are not just advantageous; they are essential for staying ahead of industry trends, mastering evolving technologies, and nurturing a mindset of perpetual growth. This chapter explores the role of education in sales mastery and the development of a lifelong learning mindset for sales excellence.

The Role of Education in Sales Mastery

Recognizing the Value of Formal Education in Sales

Formal education provides a structured foundation for sales professionals, equipping them with fundamental knowledge and skills. This section explores the value of formal education in sales mastery.

Relevant Degrees and Certifications: Delve into the significance of degrees and certifications in sales. Learn how academic credentials, such as degrees in marketing or sales certifications, validate expertise and enhance credibility in the field.

Industry-Specific Training Programs: Explore the benefits of industry-specific training programs. Understand how specialized training, whether offered by educational institutions or industry associations, addresses the unique challenges and nuances of sales within specific sectors.

Harnessing the Power of Online Courses and Webinars

Online learning platforms have revolutionized the accessibility of education. This section explores the advantages of online courses and webinars in facilitating continuous learning for sales professionals.

Flexibility and Convenience: Delve into the flexibility and convenience offered by online courses. Learn how self-paced learning, accessibility from anywhere, and the ability to balance education with professional commitments contribute to ongoing development.

Specialized Training Modules: Explore the availability of specialized training modules online. Understand how targeted courses on sales techniques, customer relationship management, and emerging technologies allow sales professionals to tailor their learning experience.

Developing a Lifelong Learning Mindset for Sales Excellence

Embracing a Growth Mindset in Sales

A growth mindset is the foundation of lifelong learning. This section explores the importance of adopting a growth mindset for achieving sales excellence.

Embracing Challenges and Learning from Failure: Delve into the concept of embracing challenges as opportunities for learning. Learn how viewing setbacks as valuable experiences and extracting lessons from failures foster a resilient and growth-oriented mindset.

Cultivating Curiosity and Inquisitiveness: Explore the role of curiosity in fueling lifelong learning. Understand how cultivating a natural curiosity about industry trends, customer behaviors, and emerging technologies propels continuous exploration and knowledge acquisition.

Leveraging Mentorship and Coaching

Mentorship and coaching are invaluable tools for professional development. This section explores the benefits of mentorship and coaching in guiding sales professionals on their learning journey.

Learning from Experienced Mentors: Delve into the advantages of learning from experienced mentors. Understand how mentorship provides insights, guidance, and real-world perspectives that accelerate the development of sales skills and strategic thinking.

Structured Coaching Programs: Explore the benefits of structured coaching programs. Learn how formal coaching initiatives, whether within organizations or through external coaching services, provide a systematic approach to skill development and performance improvement.

Participating in Industry Conferences and Events

Industry conferences and events offer immersive learning experiences and networking opportunities. This section explores the advantages of participating in such events for sales professionals.

Exposure to Cutting-Edge Trends: Delve into the exposure to cutting-edge trends at industry conferences. Learn how attending conferences provides firsthand insights into emerging technologies, market dynamics, and innovative sales strategies.

Networking and Knowledge Exchange: Explore the role of networking in knowledge exchange. Understand how connecting with industry peers, thought leaders, and experts at events facilitates the exchange of ideas, best practices, and valuable experiences.

Reading as a Continuous Learning Tool

Reading is a timeless and accessible method of continuous learning. This section explores the significance of reading for sales professionals.

Staying Informed with Industry Literature: Delve into the importance of staying informed with industry literature. Learn how regularly reading books, articles, and research papers keeps sales professionals abreast of evolving theories, best practices, and case studies.

Exploring Diverse Perspectives: Explore the benefits of exploring diverse perspectives through reading. Understand how exposure to a variety of authors, thought leaders, and genres broadens thinking, stimulates creativity, and fosters a well-rounded approach to sales.

Implementing Continuous Learning Strategies in Sales Teams

Designing Tailored Training Programs

Tailored training programs cater to the specific needs of sales teams. This section explores the design and implementation of customized training initiatives.

Identifying Team Skill Gaps: Delve into the identification of skill gaps within sales teams. Learn how assessing the strengths and weaknesses of team members guides the development of training programs that address specific areas for improvement.

Incorporating Interactive and Practical Elements: Explore the integration of interactive and practical elements in training. Understand how incorporating role-playing, case studies, and simulations enhances engagement and allows sales professionals to apply theoretical knowledge in real-world scenarios.

Encouraging Cross-Functional Learning

Cross-functional learning fosters a holistic understanding of business operations. This section explores the advantages of encouraging cross-functional learning within sales teams.

Collaboration with Other Departments: Delve into the collaboration with other departments for cross-functional learning. Learn how interactions with colleagues from marketing, product development, or customer support provide insights into broader business dynamics.

Job Rotation and Cross-Training: Explore the benefits of job rotation and cross-training initiatives. Understand how exposing sales professionals to different roles and responsibilities within the organization develops versatility, adaptability, and a comprehensive skill set.

Measuring the Impact of Continuous Learning

Key Performance Indicators (KPIs) for Continuous Learning

Measuring the impact of continuous learning requires specific key performance indicators (KPIs). This section explores KPIs that gauge the effectiveness of ongoing learning initiatives.

Skill Improvement and Mastery: Delve into the measurement of skill improvement and mastery. Learn how assessing the enhancement of specific sales skills and competencies provides tangible evidence of the impact of continuous learning.

Adoption of New Techniques and Technologies: Explore the adoption of new techniques and technologies as a KPI. Understand how tracking the integration of innovative approaches and technologies into sales practices indicates the success of continuous learning initiatives.

Feedback Mechanisms and Evaluation

Feedback mechanisms are essential for evaluating the effectiveness of learning programs. This section explores the implementation of feedback and evaluation processes.

Collecting Feedback from Participants: Delve into the collection of feedback from participants in learning programs. Learn how soliciting input on content, delivery, and relevance allows organizations to refine and tailor future learning initiatives.

Periodic Evaluation of Learning Outcomes: Explore the periodic evaluation of learning outcomes.

Understand how assessing the application of knowledge gained, improvements in performance, and achievement of learning objectives provides insights into the overall impact of continuous learning.

Continuous Improvement of Learning Initiatives

Continuous learning initiatives should be subject to continuous improvement. This section explores strategies for refining and enhancing ongoing learning programs.

Iterative Design and Implementation: Delve into the iterative design and implementation of learning programs. Learn how an iterative approach, involving regular reviews, updates, and adjustments, ensures that continuous learning initiatives remain relevant and effective.

Benchmarking Against Industry Standards: Explore the benchmarking of learning initiatives against industry standards. Understand how comparing the effectiveness and structure of internal learning programs with industry benchmarks informs strategic improvements.

Navigating Challenges in Continuous Learning

Overcoming Common Challenges in Learning Initiatives

Continuous learning initiatives face specific challenges that need to be navigated effectively. This section explores common challenges and strategies for overcoming them.

Resistance to Change and Learning Fatigue: Delve into the challenge of resistance to change and learning fatigue. Learn how addressing concerns, promoting the benefits of learning, and creating a positive learning culture mitigate resistance and fatigue.

Balancing Learning and Work Priorities: Explore strategies for balancing learning and work priorities. Understand how aligning learning initiatives with organizational goals, offering flexible learning options, and integrating learning into daily workflows contribute to effective time management.

Sustaining a Lifelong Learning Culture

Fostering a Culture of Lifelong Learning within Organizations

Sustaining a lifelong learning culture requires a commitment from organizations. This section explores strategies for fostering a culture of continuous learning within sales teams.

Leadership Support and Advocacy: Delve into the role of leadership in supporting and advocating for continuous learning. Learn how leaders who actively endorse and participate in learning initiatives set a powerful example and create a positive learning culture.

Recognition and Rewards for Learning Achievements: Explore the implementation of recognition and rewards for learning achievements. Understand how acknowledging and celebrating individual and team learning milestones incentivize ongoing development and contribute to a culture of excellence.